COMIC BOOKS AND
MANGA

Eddie Robson

 Crabtree Publishing Company

www.crabtreebooks.com

Crabtree Publishing Company

www.crabtreebooks.com   1-800-387-7650

**Published
in Canada
Crabtree Publishing**
616 Welland Ave.
St. Catharines, ON
L2M 5V6

**Published in the
United States
Crabtree Publishing**
PMB16A
350 Fifth Ave., Suite 3308
New York, NY   10118

Author: Eddie Robson
Project editor: Ruth Owen
Project designer: Sara Greasley
Photo research: Ruth Owen
Proofreaders: Crystal Sikkens,
Robert Walker
Production coordinator:
Katherine Kantor
Prepress technician:
Katherine Kantor

With thanks to series
editors Honor Head
and Jean Coppendale,
and Joe Harris.

Thank you to Lorraine
Petersen and the
members of nasen

Content development by Shakespeare Squared
www.ShakespeareSquared.com
First published in Great Britain in 2008 by ticktock Media Ltd,
2 Orchard Business Centre, North Farm Road,
Tunbridge Wells, Kent, TN2 3XF
Copyright © ticktock Entertainment Ltd 2008

Picture credits:
2000 AD & Judge Dredd © & ® Rebellion: p. 16
2002 United Feature Syndicate, Inc. Reproduced by permission: p. 8 (bottom)
3 x 3 Eyes © 1990 by Yuzo Takada. All rights reserved. Originally
    published in Japan in 1990 by Kodansha Ltd., Tokyo. Appleseed
    Hypernotes © 1996 Shirow Masamune. All rights reserved. Originally
    published in 1996 by Seishinsha. Club 9 © 1993 by Makoto Kobayashi.
    All rights reserved. Originally published in Japan in 1993 by Kodansha
    Ltd., Tokyo. Seraphic Feather © 1997 by Hiroyuki Utatane and Toshiya
    Takeda. All rights reserved. Originally published in Japan in 1997 by
    Kodansha Ltd., Tokyo. Shadow Star © 2000 by Mohiro Kitoh. All rights
    reserved. Originally published in Japan in 2000 by Kodansha Ltd., Tokyo.
    What's Michael? © 1995 by Makoto Kobayashi. All rights reserved.
    Originally published in Japan in 1995 by Kodansha Ltd., Tokyo: p. 24
Alamy: Antiques & Collectables: p. 14, 15; FocusJapan: p. 22–23; Iain
    Masterton: p. 25 (bottom); Doug Steley B.: p. 31
Julia Bax and Eddie Robson: p. 26, 27, 28
Corbis: Asian Art & Archaeology, Inc.: p. 20; Dave Bartruff: p. 1;
    Bettmann: p. 11; Mike Blake/Reuters: p. 29; Manjunath Kiran/epa:
    p. 4 (top); John Van Hasselt: p. 5
Corbis Sygma: Amet Jean Pierre: p. 25 (top)
Richard Felton Outcault, Buster Brown (July 7, 1907). Prints and Photographs
    Division, Art Wood Collection, Library of Congress: p. 8 (top)
Getty Images: Adek Berry/AFP: p. 4 (bottom); Vince Bucci. Spider-ManTM
    & © 2008 Marvel: p. 13; Nocella/Three Lions: p. 10
goldenagecomics.co.uk: p. 9
HULK. TM & © 2008 Marvel Entertainment, Inc. Used with permission: p. 12
Images © the DFC (artist John Aggs, writer Philip Pullman): p. 17
Istockphoto: cover (top left and bottom right)
Jupiter Images: p. 21
PALESTINE © Joe Sacco, art reproduced with the permission of
    Fantagraphics Books: p. 19 (top)
Rex Features: Karl Schoendorfer: p. 2; Sony Pictures/Everett Collection. TM &
    © 2008 Marvel. © 2007 Columbia Pictures: p. 6–7; Sony Pictures/Everett
    Collection: p. 18; Warner Bros./Everett Collection: p. 19 (bottom)
Shutterstock: cover (all except top left and bottom right)
The Lone Wolf & Cub © 1995 KOIKE KAZUO & KOJIMA GOSEKI. All
    rights reserved. First Published in Japan in 1995 by KOIKE SHOIN
    PUBLISHING CO., LTD., TOKYO. English translation rights arranged
    with KOIKE SHOIN PUBLISHING CO., LTD: p. 23

Every effort has been made to trace copyright holders, and we apologize in
advance for any omissions. We would be pleased to insert the appropriate
acknowledgments in any subsequent edition of this publication.

Library and Archives Canada Cataloguing in Publication

Robson, Eddie
     Comic books and manga / Eddie Robson.

(Crabtree contact)
Includes index.
ISBN 978-0-7787-3813-8 (bound).--ISBN 978-0-7787-3835-0 (pbk.)

     1. Comic books, strips, etc.--History and criticism—Juvenile
literature. I. Title. II. Series.

PN6710.R62 2008   j741.5'69   C2008-906281-7

Library of Congress Cataloging-in-Publication Data

Robson, Eddie.
     Comic books and manga / Eddie Robson.
        p. cm. -- (Crabtree contact)
     Includes index.
     ISBN-13: 978-0-7787-3835-0 (pbk. : alk. paper)
     ISBN-10: 0-7787-3835-3 (pbk. : alk. paper)
     ISBN-13: 978-0-7787-3813-8 (reinforced library binding : alk. paper)
     ISBN-10: 0-7787-3813-2 (reinforced library binding : alk. paper)
     1. Comic books, strips, etc.--History and criticism--Juvenile
literature. I. Title. II. Series.

PN6710.R57 2009
741.5'69--dc22
                                                      2008041850

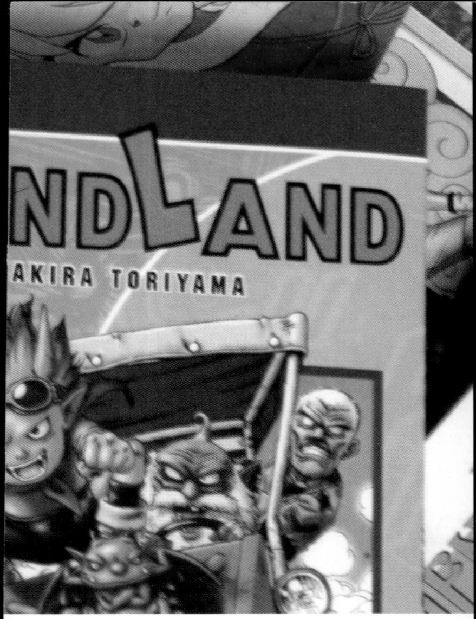
NDLAND
AKIRA TORIYAMA

Contents

CHAPTER 1

A WORLD OF COMICS

Comic books have been around for about 75 years. They are created and enjoyed all over the world. People of all ages read comic books.

A comic book artist at work in Bangalore, India.

A young Indonesian boy reads *The 99*. This comic book features 99 superheroes. They are the world's first **Islamic** superhero team.

A young Tibetan man
enjoys a comic book
about the Belgian
character, Tintin.

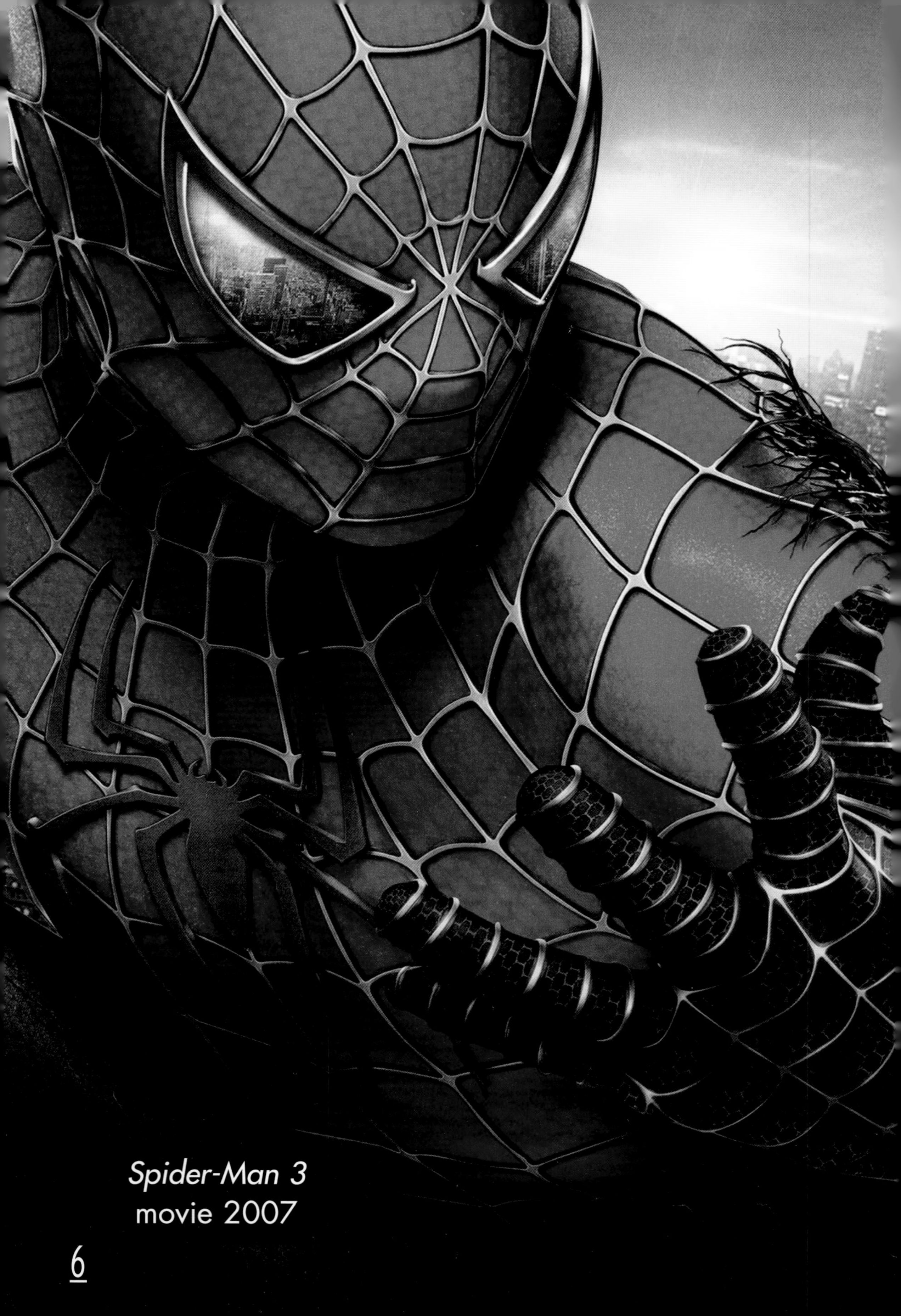

Spider-Man 3
movie 2007

Comic books have given the world superheroes such as Spider-Man and Superman.

Spider-Man is one of Marvel Comic's most popular superheroes. Peter Parker became Spider-Man when he was bitten by a **radioactive** spider.

- Spider-Man can stick to any surface
- He can lift very heavy things
- His "spider sense" warns him of danger

Comic books have also been the **inspiration** for blockbuster movies!

CHAPTER 2

THE EARLY DAYS

Comic strips first appeared in the late 1890s in American newspapers. In 1895, the comic strip *Hogan's Alley* began using the speech bubbles we still see in comic books today.

The Yellow Kid

Hogan's Alley featured a group of children living in a poor area of New York City.

One of the children, the Yellow Kid, became a huge hit with readers.

Newspaper comic strips are still popular today. Many have been running for years.

Peanuts in Spanish

Peanuts first appeared in a newspaper in 1950. Today, it is still read by 350 million people, in 2,500 newspapers, in 75 different countries!

In 1934, Eastern Colour Press published *Famous Funnies*. It was an 8-page book that re-used newspaper comic strips.

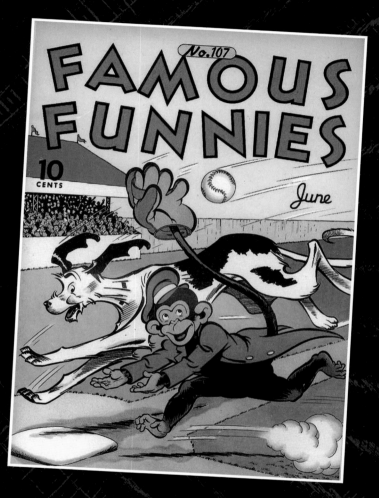

Soon, American **publishers** were producing comic books with new material. They also created new characters who appeared from one week to the next.

CHAPTER 3

AMERICAN COMIC BOOKS

In 1938, two comic book fans, Joseph Shuster and Jerry Siegel, sold some comic strips they had created to American publisher DC Comics.

The strips were about a character with superhuman powers — Superman!

Superman appeared in issue one of DC's *Action Comics.* The superhero comic book was born and...

...readers loved it!

Comic books about characters, such as Wonder Woman, Batman, and The Flash soon followed.

After a few years, crime and horror comic books became the top-selling titles in America.

In the 1950s, a **campaign** to **ban** these comic books was started in America.

Some people said comic books would turn young readers into thieves and bullies!

Some schools even held comic book burnings.

A publisher shows artwork that has been changed to fit new comic book rules.

In the end, comic book publishers set up their own strict set of rules.

Artwork was changed to be less violent. Words such as "terror" and "horror" could no longer appear on comic book covers.

In the 1960s, comic book fans were introduced to the Fantastic Four, the Incredible Hulk, the X-Men, Iron Man, and Spider-Man.

These famous characters were created by writer Stan Lee for Marvel Comics. Lee worked with artists such as Jack Kirby, Don Heck, and Steve Ditko.

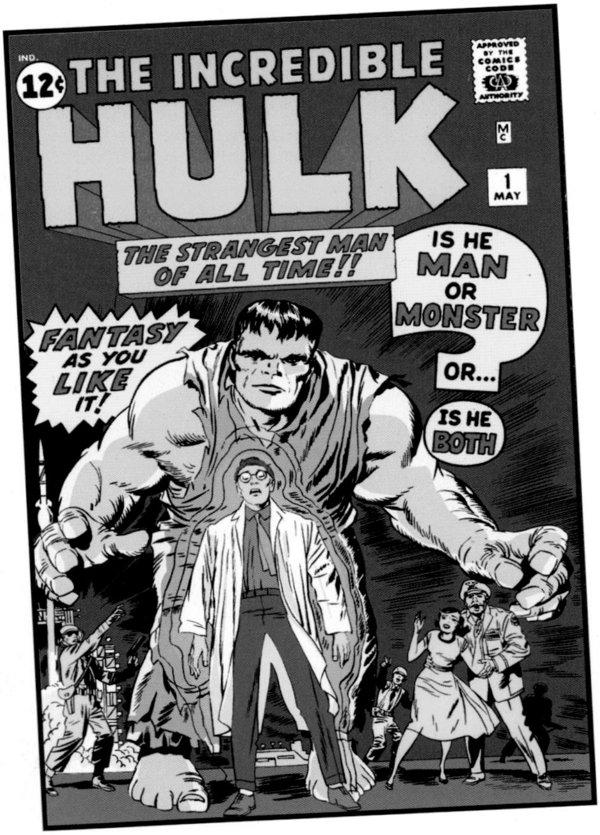

12¢
THE INCREDIBLE HULK
1 MAY
THE STRANGEST MAN OF ALL TIME!!
IS HE MAN OR MONSTER
OR...
IS HE BOTH
FANTASY AS YOU LIKE IT!

Jack Kirby's *Incredible Hulk* cover artwork

Marvel's heroes did not just fight bad guys. They also had real-life problems, such as trouble with relationships and school.

"I wanted the hero, Peter Parker, to be a teenager, and my publisher said, a teenager can't be the hero... teenagers can just be sidekicks."

Stan Lee

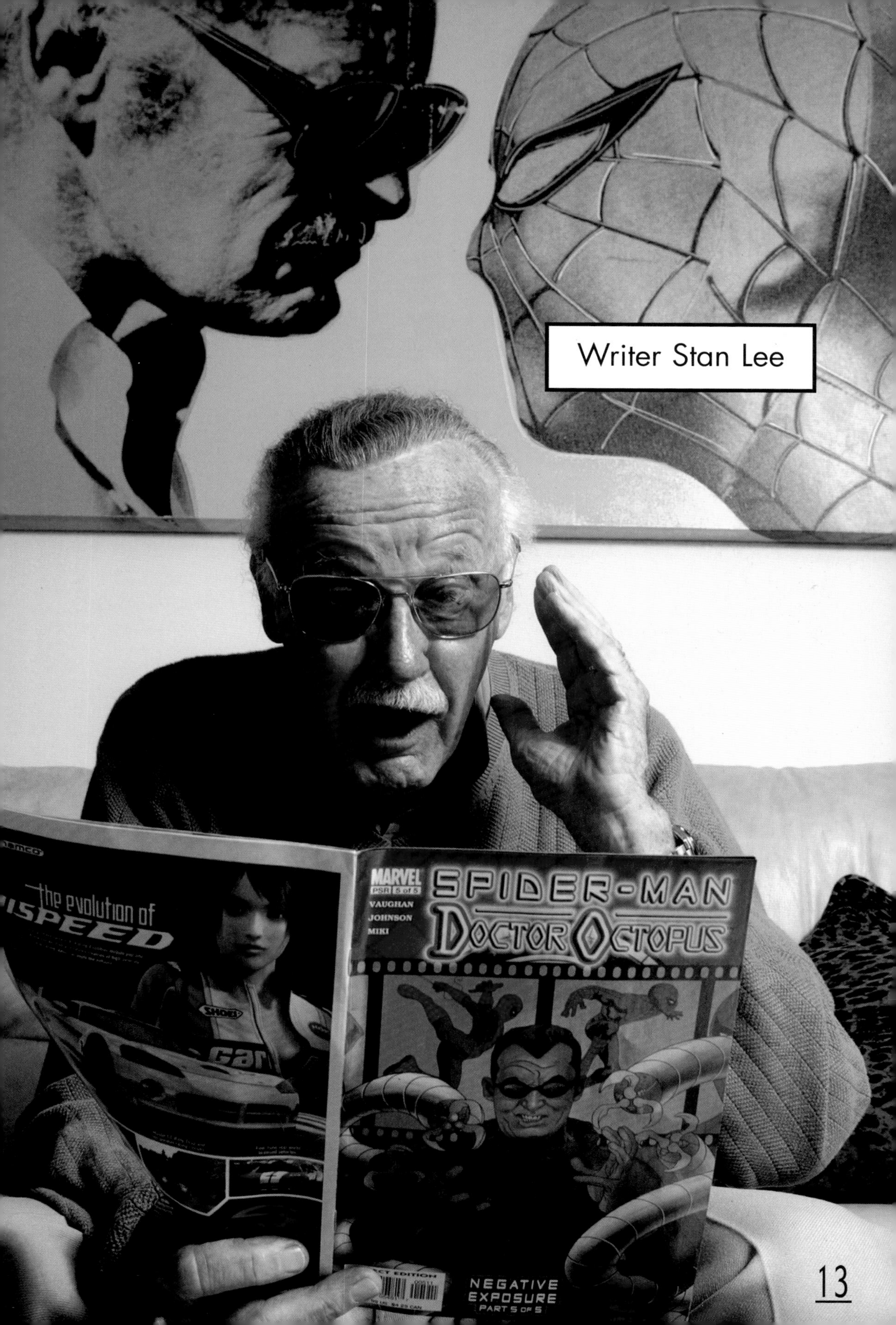
MARVEL
SPIDER-MAN
DOCTOR OCTOPUS
VAUGHAN
JOHNSON
MIKI
NEGATIVE EXPOSURE PART 5 OF 5
the evolution of

Writer Stan Lee

CHAPTER 4
BRITISH COMIC BOOKS

British comics, such as *The Beano* and *The Dandy*, were aimed at very young readers.

The Beano and *The Dandy* were first published by Scottish publisher D.C. Thomson in 1938.

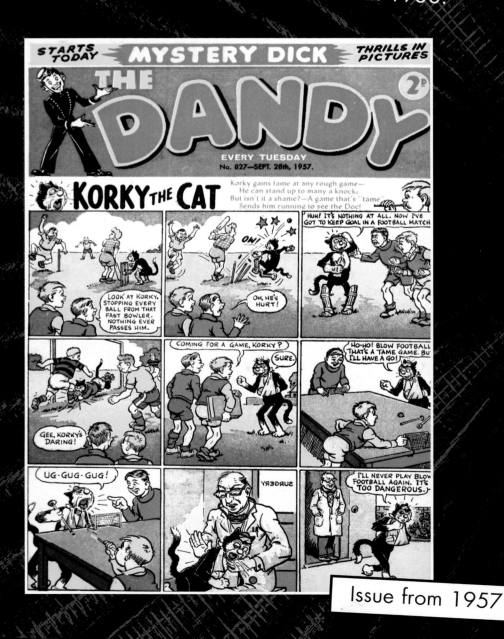

Issue from 1957

Issue from 1957

Early issues of T*he Beano* and *The Dandy* are very **rare**. This is because readers were asked to recycle their comics to save paper during World War II.

In the late 1970s and early 1980s, British comic books such as *Warrior* and *2000 AD* were published.

These hard-hitting, yet humorous comic books, were aimed at teenagers.

2000 AD introduced Judge Dredd, a law enforcement officer living in the future. In the stories, the "Judges" not only catch criminals, but they have the power to punish them, too.

2000 AD first issue 1977

2000 AD cover featuring Judge Dredd 1978

Alan Moore was one of the writers for *Warrior* and *2000 AD*.

Moore also wrote the award-winning *Watchmen*. It tells the story of a group of superheroes from the past and present. Many comic book fans think *Watchmen* is the best comic book ever.

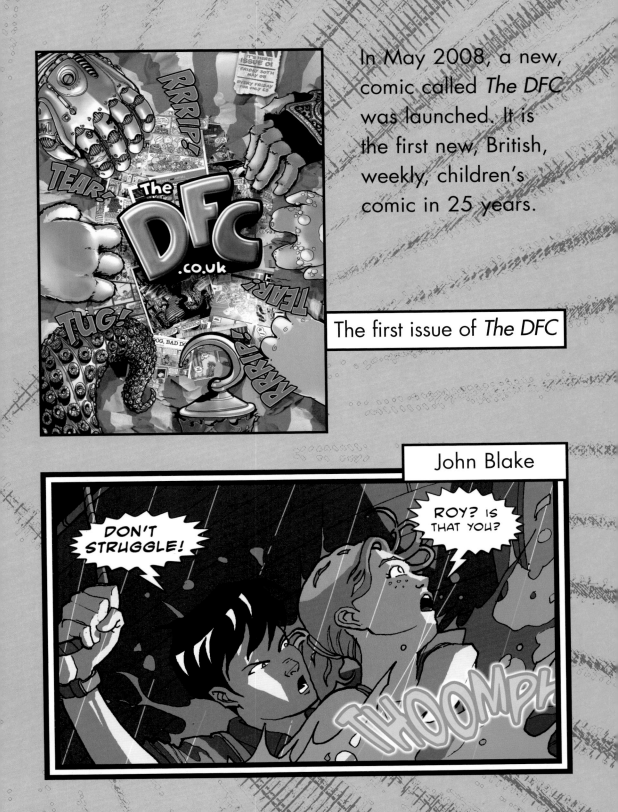

In May 2008, a new, comic called *The DFC* was launched. It is the first new, British, weekly, children's comic in 25 years.

The first issue of *The DFC*

John Blake

The DFC features "John Blake," a story written by bestselling author Philip Pullman.

CHAPTER 5: GRAPHIC NOVELS

In the late 1970s, comic book creator Will Eisner wrote and drew the first **graphic novel** — *A Contract with God*.

Other artists and writers began to create graphic novels for older readers and adults.

Today, graphic novels are available in most book stores, on many different subjects.

French-Iranian artist and writer Marjane Satrapi created the graphic novel *Persepolis*.

It tells the story of her childhood in Iran during difficult political times.

Artwork from the animated movie of *Persepolis* from 2007.

Palestine 2001

Joe Sacco is a journalist. His graphic novels present facts about situations around the world.

Sacco's graphic novel *Palestine* looks at the lives of Palestinian people living in poverty and war.

The movie *300* released in 2007

Many graphic novels have been made into movies. The movie *300* is based on Frank Miller's graphic novel about a battle in ancient Greece.

CHAPTER 6

MANGA

Japan had been producing stories with pictures for hundreds of years. Then, in the 1940s, Japan discovered comic books!

An adult picture story from 1885

After World War II, American soldiers were stationed in Japan.

When Japanese people saw the soldiers' American comic books, they quickly started to make their own comic books, known as **manga**.

Manga can be hundreds of pages long.

Now, around 2 billion manga comic books are sold each year in Japan.

People of all ages read manga. They are cheap to buy and cover subjects from sci-fi to basketball!

Readers can even enjoy manga in 24-hour cafes. They pay a small hourly fee to read from a collection of 30,000 books.

Osamu Tezuka is known as the "God of Manga."

Tezuka started writing and drawing comics in 1946, when he was still a teenager.

The wide-eyed style of some Japanese manga characters was invented by Tezuka. He got the idea from Disney cartoons.

Tezuka died in 1989. He left behind more than 700 volumes of manga. That is over 150,000 pages on many different subjects.

Tezuka took some ideas from the movies. He would often put together **panels** without words.

"Silent panels" have no words. They give a fast, dramatic flow to the action. It is just like watching a movie.

Sometimes, a manga with over 300 pages can be read in just 20 minutes.

Silent panels from *Lone Wolf and Cub* by Kazuo Koike and Goseki Kojima.

At first, manga was not well known in North America and Europe. However, in the 1980s, Japanese cartoons called **"anime"** came to this part of the world.

Anime have the same look as manga, and most artists create material for both.

Anime became popular and an interest in manga started to grow. By the 1990s, more and more manga was being **translated** into English.

The *Dragon Ball* manga was translated after the worldwide success of the anime version.

It takes a lot of work to translate manga.

Japanese sentences usually read down rather than from left to right.

Japanese books are also read from the back to the front.

CHAPTER 7
CREATING COMICS

The main jobs in the creation of a comic are:

- **Writing**
- **Pencilling**
- **Inking**
- **Coloring**
- **Lettering**

These jobs can all be done by one person, or by different people.

First, the comic is written as a **script** by the writer. The writer writes the **captions** and speech bubbles. The writer also describes what happens in each panel for the artist.

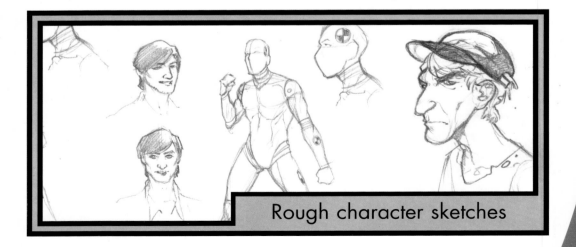

Rough character sketches

Next, the script is passed to the penciller. The penciller is the main artist on a comic.

The penciller sketches out some rough layouts.

The penciller leaves space for captions and speech bubbles.

Then, the penciller draws the final page.

Next, the inker traces over the pencil lines in black ink.

Then, the colorist adds in the colors.

The finished page

Finally, the letterer writes all the words into the caption boxes and speech bubbles.

Many comic book readers want to write or draw their own comic books.

If they cannot find a publisher, they often print and sell their own comic books. This is called self-publishing.

Comic book conventions are a good place for self-publishers to sell their books.

Fans with their goodies at a convention

Self-published manga are called "dojinshi."

At manga conventions in Japan, big publishers look for the mangaka (artists) of the future.

NEED-TO-KNOW-WORDS

anime The Japanese word for animation. It is actually the same as the English word—it has just been shortened

ban To not allow something

campaign When a group of people take action to try to make something happen

caption Text in a box placed inside a panel

comic book A book or magazine which contains stories told in pictures and words

comic book convention A meeting where comic book fans can buy and sell comics. Creators can talk about their work, and show their new ideas

graphic novel A long comic book that is created to be published as a book

inspiration The idea behind something

Islamic Describing a person who is a Muslim and follows the faith of Islam

panels The areas on a page where the artwork is placed

manga The Japanese word for comics

publisher A company that creates and sells comic books, magazines, newspapers, or books

radioactive Something that gives off harmful radiation

rare Not many of something

script A document which contains all the text which will appear in a comic book. A script for a play or movie contains all the speech and instructions for the actors

translate To change something from one language to another

MORE FACTS FOR FANS

- Most comic book fans collect comic books. Rare comic books can be very expensive. The first issue of *Action Comics,* which features Superman, is one of the world's most rare comic books. A copy in good condition is worth over $450,000!

- Japan's "Super Comic City" convention has over 18,000 booths selling dojinshi. In the U.S., most comic convention visitors are male. At "Super Comic City," most of the visitors are female.

- The internet is now an affordable way for comic book creators to make their work available. They simply put it on a website!

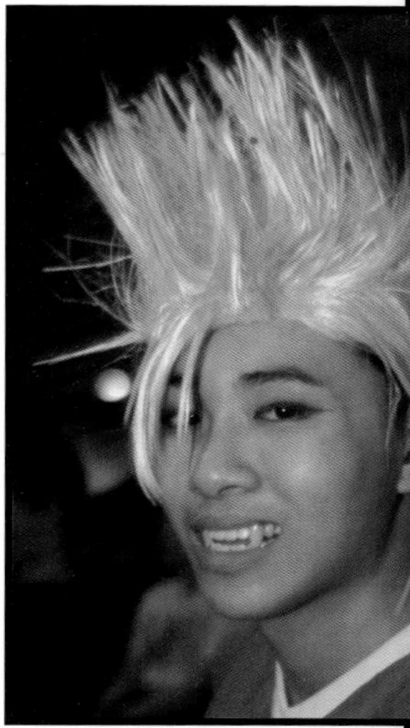

Fans at manga conventions often dress up as their favorite character.

COMICS AND MANGA ONLINE

www.comicbookresources.com
Reviews and information about comic books

http://en.tezuka.co.jp/
Learn more about *Osamu Tezuka*

www.howtodrawmanga.com
Helpful tips for drawing your own manga characters

Publisher's note to educators and parents:
Our editors have carefully reviewed these websites to ensure that they are suitable for children. Many websites change frequently, however, and we cannot guarantee that a site's future contents will continue to meet our high standards of quality and educational value. Be advised that children should be closely supervised whenever they access the Internet.

INDEX

Printed in the U.S.A. - BG